OXFORD
UNIVERSITY PRESS

 **Shipwrecks**

Madeline Samuel

Contents

Introduction 3
Shipwrecked by Overcrowding 5
Shipwrecked by Storm 6
Shipwrecked by Hurricane 10
Shipwrecked by Ice 13
Shipwrecked by War 15
Shipwrecked by Collision 18
Shipwrecked by Bomb 21
Glossary 23
Index 24

The bow of a shipwreck

Introduction

A shipwreck is a destroyed ship. Ships can be destroyed in many ways. Fires, collisions, storms and explosions are all ways in which ships can be destroyed and wrecked.

Shipwrecks are found in seas, oceans and lakes all over the world. In the past there were many shipwrecks. In modern times, there are fewer shipwrecks. This is because there are better **weather reports**. The way ships are built has also improved. Better ways of **navigating** also help keep the number of ship disasters low.

These are signal flags. They are used to send messages from one ship to another. Flags stand for letters and words.

 I must abandon my vessel

Diver exploring a shipwreck

Some shipwrecks are famous. Some have become famous because of the large number of lives lost. Some shipwrecks are famous because they are interesting places to dive down to.

Shipwrecked by Overcrowding

Mary Rose

The *Mary Rose* was built in the early 1500s. It became the flagship of the English Navy. For 34 years, the *Mary Rose* served England.

On July 19th, 1545, the *Mary Rose* set off from Portsmouth to defend England against a French invasion fleet. Only 1.5 km from shore, the *Mary Rose* sank.

The cause of the tragedy was overcrowding. There were too many men on board. Of 700 men, only 40 survived.

Raising the *Mary Rose*

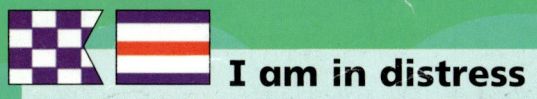 I am in distress

Shipwrecked by Storm

Whydah

In the 1700s, the *Whydah* was an English slave ship. It brought slaves from Africa to the West Indies. The slaves were sold for gold and other goods.

A pirate flag is called a Jolly Roger.

NORTH AMERICA

CUBA

WEST INDIES

JAMAICA

SOUTH AMERICA

 You are running into danger

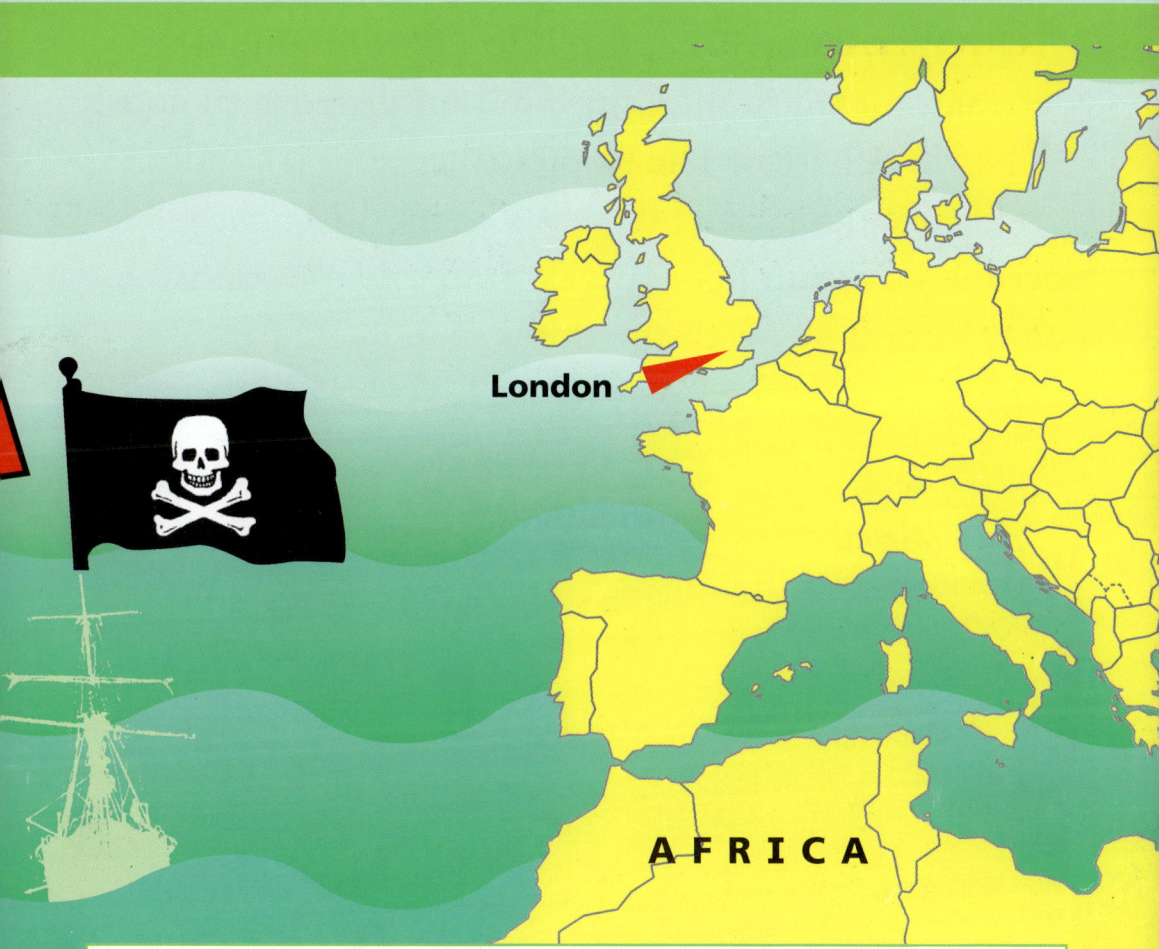

In February 1717, the *Whydah* dropped some slaves off in Jamaica. The ship was near Cuba, heading back to London, when pirates chased and captured it. The pirates were led by Samuel 'Black Sam' Bellamy. The *Whydah* was a great prize for Black Sam as it had gold, jewellery and weapons on board.

On April 26th, 1717, the *Whydah* was caught in a terrible storm just off Cape Cod on the eastern coast of North America. The ship crashed into a sandbar and broke apart. The contents of the *Whydah* spilled across the ocean floor. Black Sam and 143 of his crew went down with the ship.

Treasure recovered from shipwrecks

 **Sand bar is dangerous**

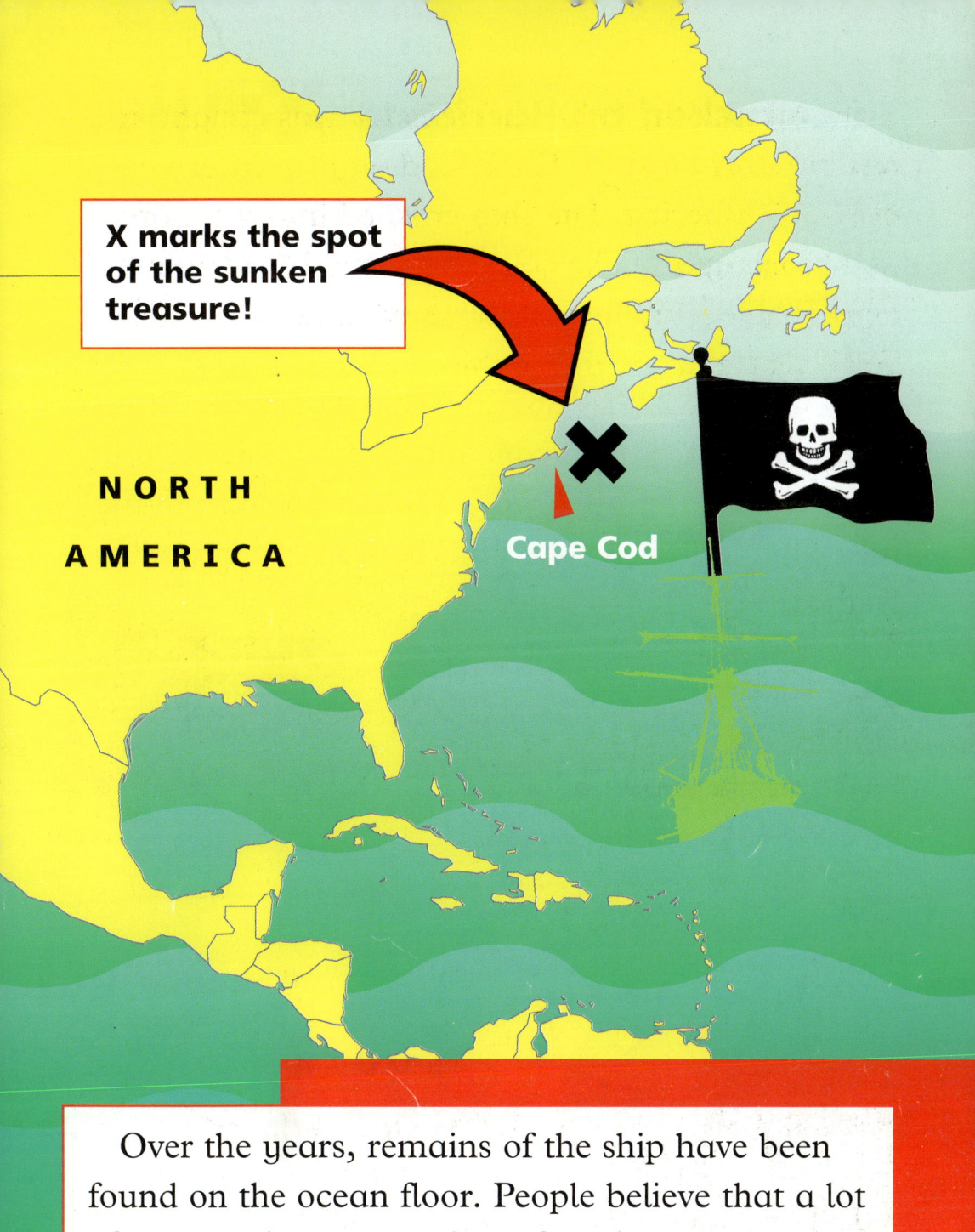

Over the years, remains of the ship have been found on the ocean floor. People believe that a lot of treasure has not yet been found.

Shipwrecked by Hurricane

RMS *Rhone*

The RMS *Rhone* was a British royal mail steamship. It carried mail and passengers from England to the Caribbean.

On October 29th, 1867, the ship was in the British Virgin Islands. A hurricane hit. The captain tried to make a break for open water. To get away from the rocks and land he headed out between Peter and Salt Islands.

BRITISH VIRGIN ISLANDS

SOUTH AMERICA

 You are in a dangerous position

Artist's impression of a ship caught in a hurricane

Then, the second part of the hurricane hit with vicious winds and huge waves. The RMS *Rhone* was slowly pushed towards the rocks. When it hit Black Rock Point the boilers exploded. The ship split in half. Only a handful of the 125 people on board survived.

Diving in tropical waters

The **bow** and **stern** of the ship now rest separately on the bottom of the ocean off Salt Island, near Black Rock Point.

Many people think that the RMS *Rhone* is one of the best wrecks to dive down to in the world. This is because it is in good condition. People also like diving there because the water is warm and clear.

Shipwrecked by Ice

Endurance

In December, 1914, the *Endurance* set sail for Antarctica. Sir Ernest Shackleton led the **expedition**.

Ninety-six km from its **destination**, the *Endurance* was trapped by ice. For nine months, the ship was trapped. The men waited on board, hoping the ship would break free of the ice.

Sir Ernest Shackleton

Antarctica

Stop instantly  Keep clear

Camping on ice masses

The *Endurance* sinks.

Instead, the ship's timbers began snapping. The crew watched from an ice floe as the *Endurance* was slowly crushed.

The men were left on the ice with three lifeboats and not much else. For months, they camped on drifting ice masses. Finally, some of the men rowed 1287 km in a lifeboat to get help. They succeeded. Not one life was lost during the whole two years.

Shipwrecked by War

Bismarck

The *Bismarck* was the most powerful warship in the German navy. On May 25th, 1941, during World War II, the *Bismarck* came across two British battle cruisers in the Denmark Strait near Iceland. The *Bismarck* sank one of these, the HMS *Hood*, then escaped.

GREENLAND **Denmark Strait** **ICELAND**

German navy warship *Bismarck*

 **I am disabled**    **I require a pilot**

HMS *Hood* in the Panama canal

Only three of the 1416 crew on the HMS *Hood* survived. Britain was devastated by the loss of lives and the ship.

The next day the British got revenge. Fourteen swordfish torpedo bombers hit the *Bismarck*. One of these jammed her twin rudders. The ship could no longer be steered.

The British ships bombarded the *Bismarck* all night and the next morning. They left it crippled.

On May 27th, 1941, the German warship *Bismarck* sank. Only 115 of the men on board were rescued.

Bombing the *Bismarck*

I require a tug   On fire; keep clear

Shipwrecked by Collision

Andrea Doria

On the evening of July 25th, 1956, the *Andrea Doria* met with disaster. The Italian luxury cruise ship was off the coast of Nantucket in Massachusetts, USA. That night, there was fog all around the *Andrea Doria*. The ship lost all vision. The radar showed that another ship was nearby. The *Andrea Doria* did not have time to change its course.

Andrea Doria listing to her starboard side

 This ship is taking on water

At 11.10 pm, the Swedish steamer *Stockholm* slammed into the side of the *Andrea Doria*. It made a 9 m gash in the *Andrea Doria*. The *Andrea Doria* slowly began to sink.

Andrea Doria sinking

Bow damage detail

The bow is the front end of a ship.

Stockholm's bow was damaged

The *Andrea Doria* had just over 1700 passengers and crew members on board. Luckily, only 52 were killed. The *Stockholm* survived the crash and helped rescue the survivors.

Shipwrecked by Bomb

Rainbow Warrior

The *Rainbow Warrior* was a Greenpeace ship. Members of the Greenpeace organisation investigate problems to do with conservation and the environment.

On July 7th, 1995, the *Rainbow Warrior* was in Auckland, New Zealand. The crew was getting ready to sail to Moruroa Atoll in Tahiti.

Auckland

NEW ZEALAND

Rainbow Warrior

Man overboard

The *Rainbow Warrior* sinking

On the night of July 10th, the *Rainbow Warrior* was blown up in Auckland's harbour. Greenpeace photographer and crew member Fernando Pereira died in the explosion.

Timeline of Disasters at Sea

Mary Rose
1545

Whydah
1717

1500 1600 1700

Glossary

bow – The front part of a ship.

destination – The place that someone is going to or being sent to.

expedition – A journey.

navigating – Planning a route or course and sailing a ship over that route or course.

stern – The back part of a ship.

weather reports – Scientific reports, which give accurate information about the weather.

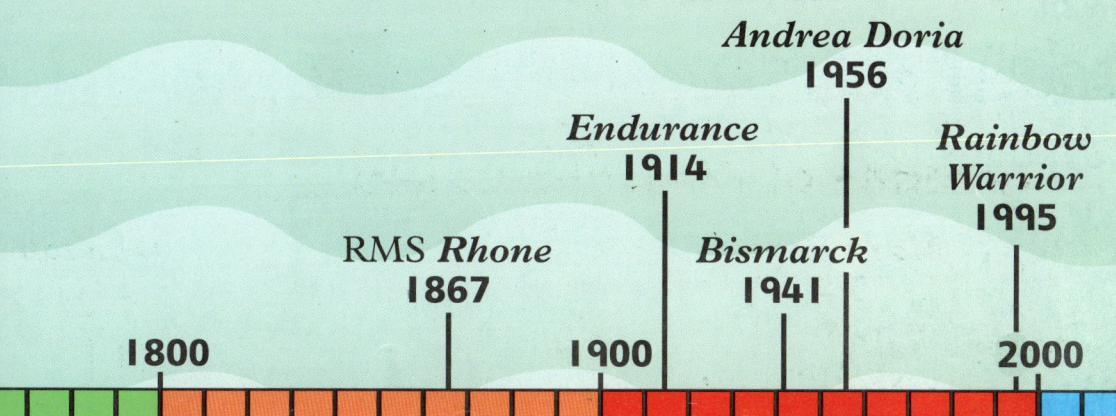

Index

Antarctica 13

disaster/s 18, 22

Greenpeace 21, 22

hurricane 10, 11

ice 13, 14

ocean/s 3, 8, 9, 12

passenger/s 10, 20

pirate/s 6, 7

radar 18

slave/s 6, 7

storm 3, 8

treasure 8, 9

vessel 3

warship 15, 17